FINDING LIGHT IN THE DARK

A HEALING JOURNEY

RISHPREET KAUR BAGGA

Contents

What Is Healing ?

Healing is a journey of recovery and renewal that includes our body, mind, and spirit. Physically, healing might involve the mending of a broken bone, the closing of a wound, or the recovery from a sickness. Emotionally and mentally, healing can be about processing and overcoming difficult experiences, such as the loss of a loved one, a breakup, or any form of trauma. This journey often requires patience, self-care, and the support of others, such as friends, family, or professionals.

Healing is not always a straightforward or quick process. It can involve ups and downs, moments of progress, and times of setbacks. It is a deeply personal experience and can look different for everyone. Some might find healing through therapy, meditation, or exercise, while others might find solace in creative activities like writing, painting, or playing music.

Ultimately, healing is about finding a new sense of balance and well-being. It's about moving from a place of pain or discomfort to one of peace and strength. It reminds us of our resilience and capacity to grow and thrive despite challenges.

This is the story of Maya's healing journey, a testament to the human spirit's incredible capacity to recover, grow, and thrive despite the challenges life may bring. Maya is a young woman who battled her fears and found a way to save herself. The one thing she came to realize along the journey is that loving oneself is more important and necessary than loving others.

1. The Breaking Point

The breaking point for a person refers to the moment when the stress, pain, or emotional burden they are experiencing becomes overwhelming and unbearable. It is the tipping point where they can no longer cope with their struggles, leading to a significant emotional or psychological crisis. This moment often triggers a deep need for change, reflection, and the start of a healing journey. The breaking point is a critical phase where the person may feel completely lost, exhausted, and desperate for relief.

As she stood at the door's threshold, Maya felt her life crumble around her. As the only child, the terrible event that claimed her parents' lives had left a gaping hole in her heart, and she had no siblings to share the grief or memories with. Every room in her house reminded her of the warmth and love that were now gone. The grief was like a heavy blanket, suffocating her and making it hard for her to breathe. Then, as if that pain wasn't enough, her long-term relationship ended suddenly. The person with whom she had planned her future was no longer by her side. The breakup felt like a betrayal, and Maya was left feeling abandoned and alone. Her heartache was relentless, filling her days with emptiness and her nights with tears.

Maya's vibrant spirit was now dulled by the weight of her sorrow. She lost interest in the things she once loved, and getting out of bed each morning felt impossible. Her friends and family watched helplessly as she withdrew, her laughter replaced by a haunting silence. Her body ached constantly, as if the emotional pain had seeped into her bones, making every movement feel like a struggle.

The nights were the worst. Maya often found herself staring at the ceiling, unable to sleep as the weight of her grief pressed down on her. Her chest felt tight, her heart ached, and the overwhelming sense of loss would leave her gasping for air. Every breath felt like a chore, a painful reminder of the life she once had.

The breaking point came one night, when Maya found herself sitting on the cold bathroom floor, clutching a photograph of her mother. Tears streamed down her face, and the pain in her chest felt unbearable, as if her heart were being squeezed. Her thoughts spiraled into despair, and for the first time, she felt completely and utterly broken. She was overwhelmed by the weight of her grief and loss.

At that moment, she was thinking. "No one knows about the pain that flows in my veins all day, aching from my head to my toes, making it difficult for me to stand, to breathe, or to do anything. Living with all this pain, people have only seen me smiling. They don't know about the pain I have been hiding, the tears I have been holding, and how I constantly tell myself to keep standing. I am trying my best to hold my pieces together, to survive just one more day, to not cry, and to have patience. I am drowning in this ocean of sadness and misery."

Gathering herself slowly, Maya made her way to her parents' bedroom. As she looked through her mother's belongings, she found something unexpected—a box full of letters tucked away in the cupboard. These letters were written by her parents to one another and to her. Maya's hands trembled as she opened the box, each letter a piece of her family's history and love, waiting to be uncovered.

Maya took a seat on the ground, opened the box, and began to read those letters.

Letter 1

"Dear Maya,

Many, many congratulations on your special day. It is your seventh birthday today. It feels like it was only yesterday that I held you in my arms for the very first time. Look at you! You're all grown up now. I wish you the very best, and I will eventually give you all of these letters. May God bless you, sweetheart. Live a long and happy life.

Love, Mom."

Letter 2

"Dear kid, regardless of gender, we love you. It's now time for us to meet. I'm your mother, and I carried you inside of me for nine months. I have protected you throughout these last nine months, and I promise to do so in the future. I am writing to you today because I am extremely happy that I will finally get to see you and embrace you. Your father will be coming here when he finishes the preparations for your spectacular entrance at home. The house was babyproofed months ago by him. We can't wait to meet you.

From Mom and Dad, with love."

Letter 3

"A baby girl is here. It appears that God has heard my prayer to have a daughter. Little one, I am your father. I asked your mother to write because I am a writer and I write screenplays for films. I believe that everyone should write down all of their memories because you never know when they can become a fantastic story. Having a daughter is something I truly count as a blessing. I would not stop you from pursuing anything, so you can become anything you want to be.

Love, Dad"

Letter 4

"Dear Maya,

I hope this letter finds you well. I wanted to take a moment to share some thoughts and advice with you as you navigate through life.

First and foremost, always believe in yourself. You have so much potential and can achieve great things if you trust your abilities and stay confident. Remember, self-belief is the foundation for success.

In your relationships, look for people who genuinely care about you. Be in the company of friends who value and encourage you. True friends will stand by you during good times and bad. In romantic relationships, seek someone who values you and treats you with kindness and respect. Love should bring you joy and make you feel secure.

Communication is crucial in all relationships. Be honest and open with those you care about, and listen to them in return. Misunderstandings can be avoided by simply talking things through.

Life can be challenging at times, but don't let difficulties discourage you. Every challenge is an opportunity to learn and grow. Keep a positive attitude, and remember that setbacks are temporary. You have the strength to overcome any obstacle.

Take care of your health, both physical and mental. Eat well, exercise regularly, and make time for activities that bring you joy. Maintaining a balance between job and personal life is important. Don't hesitate to seek help if you're feeling overwhelmed.

Education is important, but learning doesn't stop at school. Stay curious and continue to explore new ideas and experiences. Knowledge is a lifelong journey, and the more you learn, the more you grow as a person.

Lastly, be kind and compassionate. Treat others with empathy and understanding. Small deeds of kindness can have a profound impact on a person's life. Additionally, remember to treat yourself with kindness. You are deserving of the same kindness and consideration that you show to others.

Remember, I am always here for you, cheering you on, and ready to support you in any way I can. You are an amazing person, and I am incredibly proud to be your father.

With all my love,

Dad"

Letter 5

I hope you are doing well. As you continue to grow and explore relationships, I wanted to share some thoughts on what qualities to look for in a partner and offer a bit of advice on building strong, healthy relationships.

First and foremost, look for a partner who respects you. Respect means valuing your opinions, listening to you attentively, and treating you with kindness and dignity. A relationship built on mutual respect will stand the test of time.

Trust is essential in any relationship. Find someone who is honest and reliable—someone you can depend on. Trust allows you to feel safe and secure, knowing that your partner has your best interests at heart and will be there for you through thick and thin.

Good communication is the backbone of a strong relationship. Look for a partner who is open and willing to share their thoughts and feelings with you and who also values your perspective. Being able to discuss anything and everything without fear of judgment or conflict is crucial for resolving issues and growing together.

Shared values and common goals are important for a harmonious relationship. While you don't need to agree on everything, having similar views on major life decisions, such as family, career, and personal growth, will help you build a future together. Discussing your aspirations and finding common ground will strengthen your bond.

A sense of humor is a wonderful quality to seek in a partner. Life can be challenging, and having someone who can make you laugh and find joy in everyday moments will make your journey together more enjoyable. Laughter is a great way to connect and keep your relationship light-hearted and fun.

Empathy and understanding are crucial traits in a partner. Find someone who can put themselves in your shoes and offer support when you need it. A partner who is empathetic and compassionate will help you feel understood and cared for, fostering a deep emotional connection.

It's important to choose a partner who encourages and supports your growth. A loving partner will celebrate your achievements and stand by you as you pursue your dreams. They should inspire you to be the best version of yourself and help you reach your full potential.

Remember to be yourself in a relationship. You are not required to change who you are in order to live up to the expectations of others. The right partner will love you for who you are, embracing all your strengths and imperfections.

Lastly, love yourself first. Recognize your worth and don't settle for less than you deserve. You are already complete and deserving of all the love and happiness the world has to offer.

I hope these words of advice help you navigate the world of relationships. Always remember that you deserve a partner who makes you feel valued, respected, and cherished. I am always here for you, ready to support and guide you whenever you need it.

Love, Mom"

Letter 6

"Dear Maya,

Happy 12th birthday! We hope you're having a fantastic day. We want to share something exciting with you.

Remember the diary we gave you last year? You've done a great job writing in it and sharing your thoughts and dreams. It's been wonderful to see your creativity.

This year, as a special surprise, we're taking you to a film shoot set! And guess what? The story being filmed was written by Dad. Your dad's imagination is coming to life on the big screen.

We're so proud of you for finishing your diary and for all the amazing things you've written. You're a fantastic storyteller, too!

And remember that your stories and dreams are important too. We can't wait to see what adventures you'll create next.

Happy birthday, our dear daughter. We love you lots!

With love,

Mom and Dad."

Letter 7

"Dear Maya,

We want to talk to you about our hopes and dreams for your future. You're growing up so fast, and we know you can achieve amazing things. Here are some dreams we have for you:

Firstly, we hope you always stay the kind and caring daughter you are. Being a good daughter means being there for others, being loving and respectful, and making us proud every day.

We also dream of you seeing the world. Traveling is like a school where you learn about different cultures, meet new people, and see amazing places. We hope you get to explore many countries and experience the beauty of our planet.

Writing a book is another dream we have for you. You have a way with words that can inspire and touch people's hearts. Whether it's a story, a poem, or your thoughts, we believe your writing can make a difference in the world.

Finding love and happiness is also important. We dream of you finding someone special who loves and respects you—someone who makes you happy and supports your dreams.

We also dream of you following your passions and talents. Whether it's painting, playing music, or anything else you love, keep doing it with all your heart. Your talents are a gift, and we want to see you enjoy and grow in them.

Lastly, we dream of you living a life that makes you happy and fulfilled. Find what makes you excited and gives you purpose. Make a positive difference in the world and leave a legacy of kindness and positivity.

These dreams are not just ours; they are yours too. We're here to cheer you on and support you as you chase these dreams and create a wonderful life for yourself.

With all our love,

Mom and Dad."

With every word Maya read, she missed her parents more and more. However, something changed within Maya during that intensely depressing time. She came to the realization that this was not how she was meant to live. It was a turning moment, a whispered vow to herself to get herself out of this terrible place. Her journey to healing, which would put her mental toughness to the test and ultimately lead to recovery, began at this breaking point.

2. Seeking Solace

Seeking solace goes beyond just finding temporary relief; it's about actively seeking sources of comfort and support that can help soothe emotional or mental distress. This may involve reaching out to friends or family members who offer understanding and empathy, participating in therapeutic activities like journaling or meditation to process emotions, or finding solace in nature by spending time outdoors and connecting with the calming rhythms of the natural world.

It's also about creating spaces and moments in your life that nurture your well-being, whether it's through self-care practices like taking a relaxing bath, listening to music that uplifts your spirits, or engaging in hobbies and activities that bring joy and fulfillment. Seeking solace is a proactive and intentional effort to cultivate inner peace, resilience, and emotional healing during challenging times.

In the days that followed, Maya sought solace in every way she could. She began journaling, pouring her heart and soul onto the pages, hoping to find some relief in the act of writing. She picked up painting, using colors to express the emotions she couldn't put into words. Her canvases became a visual diary of her pain, confusion, and occasional glimpses of hope.

Maya also immersed herself in any activity that could keep her mind distracted from the overwhelming grief. She took long walks in nature, finding some comfort in the serenity of the outdoors. She read books, watched movies, and even tried her hand at cooking new recipes—anything that could occupy her thoughts and give her a break from the constant heartache.

In her quest for solace, she also turned to meditation and yoga, seeking peace in the stillness and gentle movements. She joined support groups, where she could share her feelings with others who understood her pain, finding a sense of community and understanding.

Through these small acts of self-care and distraction, Maya began to find tiny pockets of peace. It wasn't a cure for her pain, but it was a start. She realized that seeking solace wasn't about forgetting her grief but about learning to live with it, to find moments of respite and strength amid the storm. Her healing journey had begun, marked by the letters she had discovered and the new practices she embraced to keep moving forward, one day at a time.

Some of the things that she wrote were:

"I'm concerned about investing too much emotion in things that aren't meant for me, people I can't keep, places I don't belong, and dreams that will never come true. I am scared of emotional suffering."

"My heart cries and is slowly giving up.

What will happen next?

Am I having a heart attack?

Why am I sweating so badly, even when the air conditioner is on?

Why are my hands shaking?

Why can't I type?

What is happening with me?"

"The sunset rays are breaking through, filled with regret.

I stand beneath them, calling you, and dreams are all I get."

"To everyone out there who is fighting a battle no one knows about, You are the bravest t soul." There must have been times when you felt like giving up on everything, but trust me, it takes courage to keep going. I know there are times when you find yourself alone, even when you are surrounded by people, because you find it immensely difficult to reach out for help. No one but the mirror neatly fixed at the corner of your room has witnessed the most vulnerable version of you; the four walls of your room have heard you cry helplessly on days when you actually needed someone to embrace you and whisper, You are doing great.".

I hope at some point in your life you come across a person who never hesitates to assure you when you doubt yourself for not being enough. I hope you find someone who makes you feel heard and seen so that you do not have to trap these feelings within the pages of your notebook. I wish you never had to go to bed with a heart full of chaos and a soul devoid of happiness. I hope that in the future you discover the happiest version of yourself so that you do not have to pretend to be okay when you are not actually okay. I hope someone hears the loudness of your silence, rescues you, and magically heals you.

I genuinely want you to win this battle, not because I know how painful it is to walk down this road all alone, but because you deserve to win. You deserve selfless love, kindness, and a hug on the days when your heart breaks in silence. You are special, you are precious, you are a "WARRIOR".

PS: If all you are doing now is holding yourself together, I am proud of you.

(A well wisher)"

3. The Role of Support

The role of support means providing assistance, encouragement, and understanding to someone in need. It involves being present, offering a listening ear, and providing emotional, practical, or moral aid to help the person navigate through difficult times. Support can come from friends, family, professionals, or community groups, and it plays a crucial role in helping individuals cope with challenges, build resilience, and find strength to move forward. It's about creating a safe space where the person feels heard, valued, and not alone in their struggles.

In the days that followed, Maya found herself surrounded by an incredible amount of help and kindness from those around her. Her friends and relatives were there for her in every way possible.

Her best friend, Simran, became her rock, listening patiently to Maya's heartaches and fears without judgment. Together, they spent countless hours talking, laughing, and sometimes crying, which made her feel better.

Maya's relatives also stepped in, taking care of practical matters so she could focus on healing.

The community around Maya also played a crucial role. Neighbors brought over homemade meals, friends organized outings to lift her spirits, and colleagues at work offered understanding and flexibility. Each act of kindness and support helped Maya feel less alone in her journey.

She also sought professional help, attending therapy sessions where she could openly explore her feelings and learn coping strategies. The therapist became another pillar of support, guiding Maya through the ups and downs of her healing process.

Even in moments of crisis, when the weight of her grief threatened to overwhelm her, Maya knew she could reach out and find support. The network of care that surrounded her became a safety net, allowing her to navigate the darkest moments with a glimmer of hope.

Through the power of support, Maya discovered that healing wasn't a solitary journey but a collective effort. It was the love, understanding, and encouragement of those around her that helped her. With everyone's love and care, Maya started to feel stronger and more hopeful every day.

4. Embracing Setbacks

Embracing setbacks means accepting and learning from difficulties or failures rather than being discouraged by them. It involves recognizing that setbacks are a natural part of life and using them as opportunities for growth and improvement. Embracing setbacks means maintaining a positive attitude, finding lessons in challenges, and continuing to move forward despite obstacles. It's about seeing setbacks not as defeats but as valuable experiences that contribute to personal development and success.

But despite all this support, Maya still faced many setbacks. Each day was a battle, and there were moments when the pain felt overwhelming. She felt like she was taking one step forward and two steps back. There were nights filled with tears and days when getting out of bed seemed impossible.

Instead of letting these setbacks defeat her, Maya began to embrace them. She realized that each challenge was an opportunity to learn and grow. Every tear, every moment of doubt, was a step towards healing. She understood that setbacks were not signs of failure but necessary parts of her journey.

When she felt overwhelmed, she reminded herself that it was okay to struggle and that each setback was making her stronger.

Embracing her setbacks, Maya found new strength within herself. She learned to be patient and kind to herself, knowing that healing was a process. She started to take pride in her ability to rise after every fall.

This acceptance and learning from her challenges became a vital part of her healing, showing her that setbacks were not the end but rather new beginnings on her path to recovery.

5. New Beginning

A new beginning means starting over with a fresh perspective, leaving past difficulties behind, and embracing new opportunities and possibilities. It involves a renewal of hope, a chance to rebuild, and the courage to embark on a new path. This concept often includes personal growth, learning from past experiences, and moving forward with a stronger, more positive outlook on life. A new beginning is about transforming challenges into opportunities for growth and viewing each day as a fresh start to create a better future.

With time and support, Maya was able to cope with the loss she suffered. Her parents had always wanted her to live her best life, and she was determined to make them proud. One dream that had always been close to her heart was writing a book. It was a dream she had nurtured since childhood, a dream her parents had encouraged her to pursue. With determination and dedication, Maya poured her heart and soul into her writing. She spent countless hours at her desk, crafting stories that spoke of hope and the power of love.

And then, one day, Maya achieved her dream. Her book was published, and it touched the hearts of readers around the world. Her parents may not have been there to see her book in print, but Maya knew they were watching over her, proud of the woman she had become. She had honored their memory by living her best life, pursuing her dreams, and making a difference in the world.

Through it all, Maya never dwelled on the details of how her relationship ended. What hurt the most was that during her darkest moments, the person she had counted on wasn't there to support her. The absence during her times of need left a deep wound in Maya's heart.

Maya realized that there is no greater love than the love of parents. Boyfriends may come and go, but the bond shared with parents remains for life. This realization gave Maya strength and a renewed sense of purpose. She vowed to live her life in a way that would make her parents proud, knowing that their love and guidance would always be with her, guiding her through life's challenges.

A letter that Maya wrote to herself,

"Dear Future Maya,

As I write this letter to you, I want you to know how much you are loved and valued. You have come a long way, and I am proud of the person you have become. Remember to always cherish yourself and embrace self-love in all aspects of your life.

Firstly, I want to remind you of your worth. You are deserving of love, happiness, and all the good things life has to offer. Don't ever doubt your worthiness or let anyone make you feel less than you are.

Take care of yourself, both physically and mentally. Nurture your body with healthy food, exercise, and plenty of rest. Your well-being is important, so prioritize self-care and listen to what your body needs.

Embrace your emotions, both the highs and the lows. Allow yourself to feel deeply and express your thoughts and feelings openly. Remember that it's okay to ask for help and seek support when you need it.

Forgive yourself for past mistakes and shortcomings. We all make errors, but they do not define us. Learn from them, grow stronger, and move forward with grace and resilience.

Set boundaries that honor your values and protect your well-being. Surround yourself with people who uplift and support you, and let go of toxic relationships or situations that no longer serve you.

Keep pursuing your dreams and passions with determination and enthusiasm. Believe in yourself, and never underestimate your capabilities. You have the strength and courage to overcome any obstacles that come your way.

Lastly, always remember to be kind to yourself. Treat yourself with the same love, compassion, and understanding that you show others. You are worthy of self-love, and it is the foundation for a fulfilling and joyful life.

With love and admiration,

Maya (present self)"

Conclusion

It's crucial for people to heal from the things that are not their fault. Nowadays, many individuals bottle up their emotions, avoiding grief and pushing their feelings aside. This can lead to a loop of misery and feeling stuck. Healing is essential, especially after a relationship ends. When it comes to relationships, healing is particularly important. Ending a relationship can leave deep emotional scars, and without proper healing, these wounds can hinder personal growth and future relationships. Healing allows individuals to process their emotions, understand their experiences, and learn from their mistakes. It allows a person to process their emotions and move on with their life. Moving on doesn't mean jumping from one relationship to another; it means letting go of the memories and mistakes that hold them back and achieving emotional closure and peace. It's about releasing the past's hold on you and embracing the present and future with a renewed perspective. Without taking the time to heal, unresolved emotions can seep into every aspect of a person's life, affecting their mental health, relationships, and overall well-being. It's a necessary step to regain emotional balance, find inner peace, and be open to new experiences and relationships. Remember, healing isn't a sign of weakness but a courageous step towards a healthier, happier life. Ultimately, healing is about self-care and self-love. It's about giving yourself the time and space to mend, grow, and thrive. By embracing the healing process, individuals can break free from the cycle of pain and build a life filled with joy, purpose, and meaningful connections.

Maya showed incredible strength even after losing both her parents. She kept going, determined to make their dreams come true. Her story is really inspiring because it teaches us the immense value of a parent's love.

It's okay to feel sad after a breakup, but it's also important to remember that life goes on. When people talk about giving up their lives for love, they often mean doing something really big or even dangerous for someone they care about. But sometimes, those big gestures can end in sadness or even tragedy.

The problem is that young people might not fully understand what true love really means. They might see love in movies or on social media and think it's all about grand gestures or sacrificing everything for someone. But real love is about caring for each other, respecting each other, and making each other happy in healthy ways.

It's important for adults to help young people understand the difference between infatuation and real love. Teaching them about communication, respect, and self-care can help them make better choices in relationships and avoid getting hurt. So, while it's sad to see young people making big sacrifices for what they think is love, it's also a reminder that they need guidance and support to navigate the ups and downs of relationships.

So, we shouldn't let a breakup or the end of a relationship destroy us. Instead, we should take Maya's example and honor the time we shared with that person while moving forward with our lives.

We can't erase the memories or the feelings we had, but we can choose to cherish them while making new memories and finding happiness in other ways. Maya's resilience teaches us that we're capable of overcoming heartbreak and finding new paths to fulfillment.